Lisa Gorton | Press Release

Dear Christopher,
Lisa Gorton

New Poems

GIRAMONDO POETS

Lisa Gorton | Press Release

First published 2007
for the Writing & Society Research Group
at the University of Western Sydney
by the Giramondo Publishing Company
PO Box 752 Artarmon NSW 1570 Australia
www.giramondopublishing.com

© Lisa Gorton 2007

Designed by Harry Williamson
Typeset by Andrew Davies
in 10/17 pt Baskerville

Printed and bound by Ligare Book Printers
Distributed in Australia by Tower Books

National Library of Australia
Cataloguing-in-Publication data:

Gorton, Lisa, 1972– .
Press Release.

ISBN 978 1 920882 34 1.

I. Title.

A821.4

All rights reserved.
No part of this publication may be reproduced, stored in a retrieval system or transmitted in any form or by any means electronic, mechanical, photocopying or otherwise without the prior permission of the publisher.

For my grandparents

Acknowledgements

I am grateful to the editors of the anthologies and journals in which many of these poems, or versions of them, first appeared: *Antithesis, Antipodes* (US), *The Age, The Australian Book Review, Best Australian Poems 2004, Best Australian Poems 2005, HEAT, Poetry* (US), *Letters to Les, Quadrant* and *Vintage;* and the Red Room Company, which commissioned 'Occupied' for publication inside loo doors in Australian cinemas and airports. I am grateful to editors, such as Paul Kane and Peter Rose, who offered advice on individual poems.

    I also thank Val Creese, Chris Wallace-Crabbe, Barbara Everett and the Reading Poets for guidance and companionship. I am grateful to Antoni Jach, who read this manuscript and made useful suggestions. John Wentworth gave a great deal of time and support. Above all, I thank my editors, Ivor Indyk and Amanda Simons, for their guidance and encouragement.

    This project has been assisted by the Commonwealth Government through the Australia Council, its arts funding and advisory body.

Contents

Up in Lights

15 Graffiti
17 Beauty
18 Reflections/Federation Square
19 Occupied
20 Sci-Fi
   Space Command
   Press Release
   Evolution, 3000

The Affair

27 The Affair
28 Idyll
    Love You Bear Gifts
    Idyll
    In Winter
31 Aeroplane
32 Injury
33 Cockroaches
34 An Open Door is Not Forgiveness
35 Sleeping In

Patience

- 39 On Iona
- 41 Dean's Walk
- 42 After the Funeral
- 43 Morphine
- 45 Patience
- 46 A Natural History of Patience
- 47 Solitaire

Mallee Sequence

- 53 Petrol
- 55 Guns 1 / Major Mitchell, 1836:
- 56 Guns 2 / Old Man Piggott, 1944:
- 57 Something for Nothing, 1911
- 58 House and Home, 1944
- 59 Echo Poems / Mrs–:
  - Scald
  - Buying Water
  - Idyll, Lake Charm
  - Dust Storm
- 64 Childhood
  - Rising
  - Nag
  - Playground
  - Roll Call
- 69 Selection
- 70 Murray River Poem

Up in Lights

Graffiti

I wonder this wall can bear the weight of such words
GRAFFITI ON A WALL IN POMPEII

The city is smaller than you expected.
Its houses turn their backs on streets –

> And given half a chance
> who wouldn't bunker down behind a stack of silence?
> An arm's length of wall permits any depth of
> meditative calm or your money back –

Its walls are made of potsherds, broken bricks and stone
cut from the hill's mouth, chain-lugged to the city –

> It happened just as you picture it:
> slaves bent double against the weight, whip cracks and flies,
> that crowd in the marketplace breaking off mid-sentence
> to see peace dragged in as a pile of stones –

The stucco of the city walls is everywhere
scratched with these piss-riddled importunities –

> – Cruel Lalagus, why don't you love me?
A wall can bear the weight

    – All the girls love Celadus the Gladiator
The weight is nothing to the wall
    – Caesius faithfully loves M[... name lost]
A wall can bear the weight
    – For a good time, turn right at the end of the street.

Out of the dark, ashes fall softly.
We have to stand up again and again to shake them off.
What a weight of light!
The dark is smaller than you expected.

Beauty

Challis Avenue, 5 a.m.

The art dealer promises a flower market

> It rained in the night. The street
> lights envy themselves in asphalt
> the way Elizabeth Taylor might
> watch 'A Place in the Sun'

and the names: iris, star magnolia

> I came from sleep to the still dark.
> It is always day in dreams but the night
> has secret hours when cars drive
> into their lights like the idea of success

blazon the air, all neon expectation where he comes:

> balding, rapacious, his eyes like
> hands, his aficionado smile,
> Whiteleys in his suitcase, Bromleys in his suite
> and all the city's flowers in his palm.

Reflections / Federation Square

These winter skies create themselves like a future:
ruined cities overrun with light,
with pale-haired warriors pillaging, hoarding.
                These victory and bonfire skies

Make ideal companions now you're drinking
behind glass, let's not say drunk
but life is a waiter at your elbow, discreetly
                offering its à la carte.

At dusk, the city meets itself in mirrors.
Its river lights glamorise your face,
another pale flare in the dark-backed glass:
                its constellation nostalgia.

The waiter sets your plate down and you eat.

Occupied

Graffiti from a public toilet in Federation Square

Listen. We can talk here,
this republic in your empire of intention.
Whenever you close this door again
corridors will take you
as if they knew the way and could explain
but the unending rhetoric of transit
returns to the cubicle NO:
this upright casket where you sit
like the soul of a wall or buried vestal
in the aloneness of your life –
that lustre on tiles no graffiti confide.

Sci-Fi

I Space Command

Fold-out evenings, chairs in the street.
Side by side, we're making out the satellites
which like stars, like Clint Eastwood,
ride impassive through our networks of desire.

Don't be afraid. The air is full of frequencies:
a stranger dying to confide
in the ideal democracy of aerials.
It is always speaking. Do not feel alone.

All our lives, Voyager's Pioneer
carries its azimuth into the silence
made of dark, alone as metal
and still sending its signal back.

On its phonograph it bears the cast-off voices
of our childhood, saved in one-and-zero code:
'Greetings to you, whoever you are. We have
goodwill towards you and send peace across space.'

II Press Release

To honour the Year of Perfected Vision, in 2020
the PDK-4 Corporation signed up its first
Hibernation Astronaut for the missile, 'After Life',
launching its Perpetual World campaign:
'Preserving Our Most Beautiful Offspring for the New Life on Titan...'

    They chose my child. I visit him
    daily in the tiled room. His naked skin
    looks backed with ice. I see his heart
    beat hourly on the screen. He is safe,
    I know, for his will be an innocent world,
    conquered in peace.
                        He does not breathe
    more than once a heartbeat. My own
    small breaths haunt the cold when I speak
    into the audiofile they have contracted to play
    across his light years on repeat. 'Don't be afraid,'
    I say. 'Like a handshake, palm to palm,
                  a gentleman's agreement,
    your heartbeat tenders you – Are you cold?
    Listen, out of these bypassed years,
    silence in your mouth, you will amass such –

Only to think of you, falling from your name for sky
in this astonishing vessel!
      Press release, my darling,
and do not sorrow. Do not once sorrow.
If you will think of me, think only of these years
I held your unfailing present in my empty hands.'

III Evolution, 3000

In case you see history as sheer loss –
a speeding ticket two weeks later in the mail –
the future's visiting bearded archaeologist finds
alum in the fossil jaw of your Cenozoic skeleton.
'The Missing Link?' makes headlines
on New Titan.
                    But do you remember
how we swatted flies in the balding shade
a morning's walk from launch?
Their ships made a mirage fall,
our ozone crashed about our ears and we stood
mesmerised in all that falling light.

The Affair

The Affair

Our last illicit weekend,
a little tired and driving
to some Blue Mountain
getaway or other.
On the motorway
it is the car that overheats
                    whoosh
I think a whale is
caught in our engine.
We wait in the car
trying to feel
absolute about each other.
They all drive past.

Idyll

I Love You Bear Gifts

In tribute I return you seas
set in coral and current intricacies,
all the sands I can remember and
easterly winds tied in narrow trees.
World! New world of touch!
And I, like every traveller, bring too much.

II Idyll

In the garden, this pale mist,
every leaf and blade of grass
bearing quietness.

You are still inside asleep
and everything I look on seems
like something from your dream.

Even that spider in its web of light
for so I am in your design
with all its gifts none of mine.

III In Winter

Winter-
bare trees: thoughts on a vague sky.
We walk on such leaves and the gentle lies
we told those days now drift a little way
and then subside.
There is consolation in this season
or something else: call it resignation
to the cold beginnings of good-bye.

Aeroplane

The plane is still on the tarmac but already
every last thing is falling away.
Soon I'll be flying over the weather and daily
machinery of our lives together. The doors are closed
and we have all switched off our mobile phones.
I tell myself no one can come with news now,
good or bad, though I know this is not strictly
true: there's a satellite phone in my remote control.
Already, that unaccountably intimate smell
of airline food. The plane takes off and carries us
into the perpetual fact of sky. People are still
watching people talking on their TV screens
while out my window, banked clouds thin to stratosphere –
to air not shining but all the same, made of light.

Injury

for Maria Takolander

Not how it happened and not the pain.
Only the sight of it, splinter plunged in quick:
the knot and cut-swerve of wood grain
staring out my blind-eye-coloured nail
to its half-moon cataract. Only where it arrowed in
at the tip, there swelled this plush,
slow as astonishment, till the mind said: Injury.
Easy enough to take the splinter out.

Cockroaches

for Anthony Lawrence

In your night kitchen they vanish:
rewound film, its scratches and feelers,
          feelers and scratches.
Now patient in skirting boards,
hollow walls, false-bottomed cupboards,
          warm electricals,
the small and dreamless apparatus of hunger
waits, simplified and inconsolable.

An Open Door is Not Forgiveness

This door was cut from a purpose-built forest:
eucalyptus obliqua, whose leaves –
the wings of dragonflies fossilised in slate –
make no wrung-hand sound, and though
a high wind open in them sudden passages of light,
they do not fall.
                      They have their airy landings still,
their spiral stairs in mote parquet, and if
in the dry basement of their impossible walkways
I wait and listen, I hear the high-
heeled footsteps of what we passed up
hurry away.

Sleeping In

Morning starts without us.
On the wall above our pillow the window's reflection
holds itself in place like a dream's placard,
remaking even the wind out there, cut from the first ice on
    the hills,
into a decorative impulse:
its branch and leaf shadows not shining but all the same
shaking out light.

Waking is finding ache-
shaped bones, flesh weighed with sleep,
in the dent of warmth we have pressed into our mattress;
picturing with still closed eyes the suburb's damp-bright
    streets
after last night's rain:
torn clouds and more light on the asphalt
than we could find in the sky.

Sleeping in:
hours spent like holes in our pockets, thrown out
to find our way into that field which is not there
in the wall behind us – the window's idea of itself
all a matter of light –
now printing itself across our faces as we sit up
into a second chance.

Patience

On Iona

I have climbed the stairs of the tower again,
balancing on their stone hub:
                vertigo's idea of time.
Doves in the scriptorium. How they start up.
Their wings plead,
                unilluminated words
over the wheel of our endeavours: these tilled fields
and then the rock
                and then the turning sea.

Out of all sight of land this stone place,
the wide storm's
                only rain-keeper,
is the colour of tolerance, being all days
wind-eaten,
                mocked by sea-skimming birds,
and we plant our crops in strewn sea-weed
 and our bread
                tastes of scant salt ground.

I have climbed into the circle: at this height,
wind hollows the silence out
                        and gives it form
the way low clouds along the sea's edge

        mass shadowed cliffs
                and I could walk upon them –
waist-deep
            in their dove-neck colours,
            in their down, and down.

Dean's Walk

i.m. Kathy Wilkes

You wake again in your armchair,
face to a window full of winter's pale,
its juniper-tinted light and you drink it in
because it is not bitter,
not at all, not after the first bitter glass.

In the courtyard, you walk guessingly,
steered by small changes in the light
across your left cheek: leaf-shadows
and the sudden dark –
a thrum – of clouds, which passes.

In this fashion, you walk back and forth
three times before the Common Room
bay window like a cloud
shadow yourself, casting its pause upon the talk –

But let that be a dark you have left behind
in your going after the last light you can find,
                                       as far as it will go.

After the Funeral

So we walk through this cockatoo morning
surprised at the strangeness of grief
these staring cattle the husky
beige and green uncaring hills
knowing they are still and only we carry you
for like weather we fall and fall.

Morphine
i.m. Ethleen King

i
You're slumped in your lunch tray,
corn soup gunked in your new-curled hair,
spilling from the tray and *thop pthop-pthop* –
in clammy handshakes –
meeting itself distractedly on the floor.

There's a triangle of bread, one
corner bitten out of it, buttered to your cheek,
and your false teeth an inch from your mouth
as though we've sprung them *clack clackety-clicking*
into the soup in their imperturbable hunger.

ii
The soup is smooth under our nails,
bland on our tongues, is everywhere –
until the nurse brings a towel
and smears you clean awake.
Then, out of that blank we had thought death,
you sit up and eye us coldly: 'I have no future.'

iii

Say we are fires so lit with ourselves we burn bewilderedly
because the world is made of things indifferent to fire.
There we are ranged in chairs half-circling you
propped in that white bed winched too high –
a contraption of pulleys and levers the nurse works
with an adeptness like contempt – and we say nothing,
nothing, and leave at the end of visiting hours.

iv

So call this a prayer for morphine:
that it soothed the sheet,
that it held your hands in the vein,
that its fingers were light
that drew you in, like a drawing-in of breath,
and did not let you go.

Patience

Stairs that rise to unused rooms, their amber afternoons:
hours that bear the weight – mahogany as patience –
of a bed made smooth and leather-bound books sequestered
like shoes queuing – the wrong way – to step out;
goods that wait in dressing-table drawers,
pink shimmer lipstick stubs, a sunset blush,
your hair still tangled – fast – in tortoise shell,
a silver compact – of flesh-coloured dust.
Rooms as expectant as looking glass. Even their windows
waiting for you – to step into air and speak.

A Natural History of Patience

Off Eden, 1891. The lost harpoon man, Bartley,
is cut from the breathing belly of a slaughtered whale.
Flensed for blubber, ransacked for verdigris,
it yet brings forth by strange C-section
this bleach-eyed and unremembering man:
his fingers without prints, acid-eaten to a caul-skin,
and his burnt-bright, his quicksilver-coloured hair.
Out of the lagan deep, the all-dark place, this one
returned to haunt the slaughteryard, repeating
till they will be pleased at last to bury him: 'Nothing is lost.'

Solitaire

i.m. Bettina Gorton

i
After lunch on sunstruck
afternoons I look for you
in the shaking out of light
from petrol haze –

I look for you on the combed
lawns of commuter suburbs
between the hedge and standard roses
with your back to the street –

When I come home from winter
holidays I can tell you have been there,
drinking window after window of light
till it is emptied and grey –

I think once I saw you
walking the curve of a disused rail line
where the track shrugged off its sleepers
and climbed into the heat –

ii
However early we woke, you were already waiting,
slippered in dawn's sedated light,
a first glassful of distance in hand and the cards set out
with the sound of somebody closing in: step step step turn,
step step turn, step turn, turn, only you had already gone
along paths of smoke into the smoke-coloured ways
where in place of footsteps, only ash falls followed you.

Because mallee scrub is the colour of thirst
with an infrastructure of patience,
you'd been divining a path across it ever since you sat down
on the screened-in verandah in that drought at war's end
and found even burning days would upholster you in stillness,
and nights antimacassar your hair till you could rest without stain
upon the fine print of promises.

iii
Out of smoke you came walking. Your face
made a cloud in that cloud-haunted absence
over the courtyard parterre where our noon
shadows snagged on our heels, planning to lengthen.
Then somebody saw the time and we left for the wake.

Mallee Sequence

Petrol

Straight roads, built for driving fast.
You get out of winter in a day.
These paddocks so like thoughts you travel past
string out beside your asphalt purpose.

You get out of winter in a day.
Cattle fat as history watch you pass,
strung-out beside your asphalt purpose:
these vast effects of corroded light.

Cattle fat as history watch you pass
with the blank stare of what you don't remember:
corrosive effects of this vast light,
the golden relic of a dream rush.

With the blank stare of what you don't remember
a pub, a petrol station and a store –
the relics of a gold rush dream:
something so patient you might call it peace.

A pub, a petrol station and a store.
You fill up. In the sudden quiet you hear
something so patient you might call it peace:
crickets like an electric fence in the grass.

You fill up. In the sudden quiet you hear
paddocks so like thoughts you travel past:
crickets ticking electric fence sounds in the grass
and straight roads, built for driving fast.

Guns 1 / Major Mitchell, 1836:

'Wild birds rise before us,
making the noise of a multitude clapping hands.
The men fire, fire again.
Still the wild birds rise, they rise clear out of range and
where they were they leave
such wakes of light, they are tearing the blue-black
shadows out of the river –
their wing-tumult is shadows escaping air. Act
flung back to motives,
they arc away from us and scatter till I am fierce
for what I cannot remember
and still they rise, the vault is dark with their applause.'

Guns 2 / Old Man Piggott, 1944:

'Know what a punt gun is?
Struts, strapped mallee planks
and a rig of guns, double-ranked
like a two-stall choir –

Take it out in the still dark.
Night is an inch off lake
where the birds ease up and back on waves
like small breaths in and out –

One trigger slams you back
on your hands and knees in wing-
bewildered air, night mangled
all in scraps like pleas –

So you row the punt back, with one
shot you've swagged at least a hundred birds.'

Something for Nothing, 1911

The Director of the Lake Charm Irrigation Company
wears a bow-tie all drought summer like a straight-faced wink.
His promises make allotments.
He whispers: 'That's not a vanishing point. That's the world
pouring itself through the eye of a needle –
because it is right
to admire a plant that takes what it will
to make in any soil such green, acrylic and perpetual,
for the fruit gathers light to itself, leaves the dark alone.'

House and Home, 1944

On the side verandah Mrs– takes another slice of
letting herself go. Flyscreens make the kindest shade.
They are all gone to history. Paddocks walk about the house.
The house is still in the family. Memory is
small-handed creatures, they unravel shadows down
corridors, in drifting rooms. A neighbour calls at the door.
How politely it comes in, the future –
padding across the boards in soft-soled shoes
till her armchair presides over dunes and swales.

Echo Poems / Mrs–:

I Scald

'Midday like a theory of heat: dry, immaculate
but for a low craze – what the neighbours call
waters of illusion – a foot up and sideways over that
sunk flat back of Sporn's. A useless scald.
Sometimes I harvest salt there.
If they stood here they'd see me wading into that sheer of light,
up to the waist in shining blank
as though I could fossick in the full wreck of existence: a bright
dark torso signalling back.
And they fire guns at it.
Crack! and it shards, it shows the blind dirt it scathed
to make this version of an afterlife:
light drawn in to the idea of light, all-eye and all-
forgetting, more entire than perfection.'

II Buying Water

'Dust comes after things with its silent chant –
all but the cranes. They lift off the dam's mud sheen
as if their wings had nothing to do with flight.

I would have said the water truck was
carried on dirt tides over the jolting paddock
and it was the light making that metallic complaint,

that the reasoning cogitations of its pump
had nothing to do with that canvas gullet of water
filling the dam with something like invective.

But it doesn't fill. He blames the walls for cracks.
We hear it, retreating into underground caverns
with the murmurous hush that secret lovers make –'

III Idyll, Lake Charm

'To step into the lake:
to leave versions of me in shatters of light,
knee-deep in the weed
touches of what I have forgotten till I
meet the slant part:
what starts from a flaw in water, unsunned,
greenish, strung with trapped
baubles of air as if more than parallax
kept me from it:
all my errors washed out there.'

IV Dust Storm

'Slump and heft, slump and heft:
the neighbours, shovelling sand from the kitchen.
Another dust storm slouched out of afternoon
   – out of the horizon-paddock
      over Twin Dams, dry, and Sporn's Bore, indifferent
      over our drought-thwart crop of wheat:
      acres cleared in promise
      where I raked the sticks in rows, burnt off all night
      weeping for smoke,
      where I walked down hours of dark between those fires.

Slump and heft to the wheelbarrow's shudder-run
and that sound like the echo of a sound, which is distance
poured on the house-paddock, compacted sand
   – out of the unclaimed land I hold in mind
      as the lost existence of our acres:
      dunes fumbling free of the small-fingered heath
      the way the mind says *almost, almost* but the name is gone
      into the idle, the whipstick-covered plains
      the neighbours call rabbit-haven and walk with guns –

All still and haze, this hour left over, dust stacked up
the other side of shadows reaching from the fence posts,
drabs of gum. This time I watched the storm come
   – visual static the scale of din. The way
     a radio cuts out, the afternoon went out of range:
     paddocks lost and held in piled-up noise
     until this hour when haze,
       shaking off unmeaning, settles on the roof
         in sounds so small and many they might be husks of rain.'

Childhood

for my father

I Rising

Fist-eyed clean-yawner, you go
poking toes into the first light, grit-dry
drought light fuzzed with shade
on the screened-in verandah,
ankle-deep in night
arm-deep in quiet –

Shadow-scuffing door-slammer, you go
cobweb-kiting up the back paddock,
sockless in loll-tongue boots cut from the balded hide
of Heggan's worn-down cow,
now a sand-drift
nosing at the heels of its paddock-eating future –

Pot-bellied hungerer, you go
first thing to the rabbit traps, along
scribbly tracks into dunes that break
over the back paddock in a wash of rust weed
and small grass, its seeds
catch at your shins and the Bathurst burr nags –

Skinny-wristed end-maker, you go
lightly across the night-plunged sand, the hand-
held existence springs
acres in your palm until you crack! its neck
and turn for home, weighing in your arms
this shilling pelt for the rabbit-oh –
                        Because O-U-T spells out so out you GO

II Nag

Double-dink, meaning clutch and bicker,
on the pinch-withered roan, your snitch-tailed
forelock-shrugger, lank as rags, stare-
coated as a rust stain, its rump sticky-
tarred with flies starter-motoring to dunk
all woozy in its drizzle-eye. Ears
back and pegged to umbrage, it goes dig-
dig at air with its blunt-spade nose,
handle-necked in its jog-trot, trip-
jolt, its sand-slippered clip-clop
shaking out a blank, a blankety blank
makeover for the road. Go tell the roan
day-long loose-shackled to the school fence,
turn-tailed to the wind and bucket-deep in forbearance.
                      Because 1 2 3 you are not HE

III Playground

Hide and seek. Hold your hands against your eyes.
The dark is soundless reverb. You're filching
splay-fingers of light, scraps of playground
waterish with glare. It's not cheating
if you can't see anyone. They are already gone,
pocketed in quiet, world drawn back from you alone.

Counting into it again is akin to walking
over the jetty's sway-backed shadows on the lake,
shadows you have watched, belly-down on splintered heat,
some days almost to sleep, pressing your fingers
into their sudden cold till it was almost implausible:
ten steps back to the bank and drift of standing ground.

Now you're calling numbers into air like steps
and they'll carry you back to open light,
back to that first blink-eye
when so many small flares, scattering bright,
so many fires lit upon themselves,
die back and become all that was and is
                            Coming, ready or not.

IV Roll Call

Needlings, little goads in rows,
they tip their faces up, blank as knees
these gum-eyed morning gobblers,
kindling scrabblers, run out of head-
high scrub and wash-your-hands
to sit out mothers' peace, waiting
in their whole lives, their home-
made shoes, and answer: Here, Here, Here.

Selection

'Only to sleep one night at the survey peg
among the patient materials of profit –
already the fire is fast hands buying the dark –
while plovers call in these latent paddocks
and further off, a mopoke owl hunts up the quiet.'

Wall made of mallee root:
it stands – though there is just
house enough for air to be
furtive, for corner piss-stench and
danked fires.
Dust chafes the citrus, rusted vine.

Still, tourists of forlorn find themselves
lee-side of what worked this
out of Acres of future, scrub
to wreak days in, decades cleared
with fire and an axe.
Selection, heft burl by burl to the fact.

Murray River Poem

for Les Murray

Rivers start the way dreams turn into morning
as early rain makes the sound of days commuting:
song of the soft-shoe horde for idlers and layabouts
with the sound of stilettos window-shopping
whenever leaves feed their pure ideas to shadow:

> Out of Kosciusko near Mount Cobberas
> past Khancoban, out of the high places,
> from the hunter's long raging hunger –

But it is not its names the river repeats as if
trying to memorise something. It is made of fingers that
hold you in the current of forgetting and what it collects:

> Anabranches, scrolls, meanders,
> billabongs and backwaters, shoals
> or shadows, snags, a taste of vegetable decay –

Some rivers travel as the subconscious of light
but our one big river is dirt-coloured and
deliberate. And where it goes
in straight canals through the Mallee plains,
it is as we imagine forbearance to be.